GATEWAYS TO SNOWDONIA

Gateways
to Snowdonia

Michael Senior

Cover design: Eirian Evans

First edition: 2011
Gwasg Carreg Gwalch, Llanrwst
☎: 01758 750432   ▤: 01758 750438
✆: lona@carreg-gwalch.com
Website: www.carreg-gwalch.com

Contents

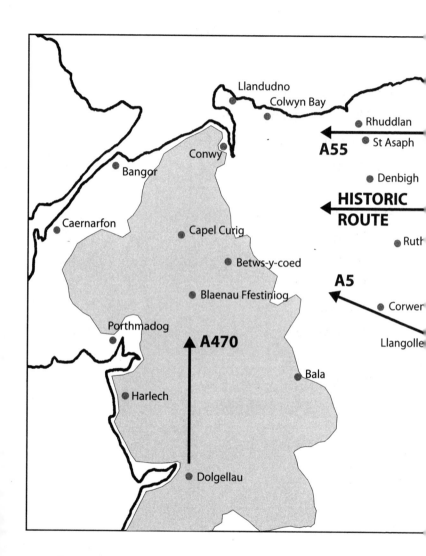

Llandudno
Colwyn Bay
Rhuddlan
A55
St Asaph
Conwy
Bangor
Denbigh
HISTORIC
ROUTE
Caernarfon
Ruth
Capel Curig
Betws-y-coed
A5
Blaenau Ffestiniog
Corwen
Porthmadog
A470
Llangolle
Bala
Harlech
Dolgellau

I   The Background

The heart of 'Pura Wallia'

The inner heartland of Wales is easily identified. The heaped-up masses of the mountains are visible from a far distance and their bulk blocks all but a few ways of approach. This geological fact, as so often, became a historical condition. Independent Wales, known in the Middle Ages as *Pura Wallia*, was easily contrasted with the Normanised southern coast, stretching to the heart of England at its border, which was known as Marchia Wallia. Independent Wales in the thirteenth century was the territory ruled over by Llywelyn the Great, the kingdoms of Deheubarth, Powys and Gwynedd. What is now known as Snowdonia is, and always was, the inner citadel, the fastness at the heart of Gwynedd.

The accident of it being marginal land operated historically in two coinciding ways. It was of less interest to an invader, and at the same time it was much easier to defend – compared to the long level coastal strip, for instance, or the broad flat sedimentary uplands stretching to the Cheshire plain. This combination favoured a type of strategy which in turn encouraged a specific mode of agriculture. When the flatter lands were overrun from beyond the Welsh border, as they frequently and easily were, the population could retreat into the hills, provided only that they could take their means of livelihood with them. Thus the herding of cattle and sheep have become the traditional form of farming, and such crops as were required for the nation's diet had to be confined to Anglesey, itself protected from Wales's borders by the mountain fastness.

As result of the security offered by the terrain much more has been preserved than the land's precarious ownership. An independence of mind has survived there to some extent untouched by invasion, a way not just of doing things but of viewing them, preserved (as cultural inheritance often is) through the tenacious medium of the language.

Lines of approach

For a long time the response of outsiders to this unrelenting heartland was to find not ways into or through it, but ways round it. The earliest signs of invasion, no doubt coming from the Irish Sea, occur at the coastal edges. Signs of penetration inland are rare, and only in two areas have we evidence still of ancient travellers: across the hills above the Conwy valley, perhaps because precipitous crags blocked the shore at Penmaenmawr, a route was found to give access to the western coast; and through the hills behind Harlech the coastal colonists seem to have carved a line of communication with the world then developing further inland.

The Romans used one of these routes, when they came, attesting to its efficiency. They built a road across the hills through the pass between Tal y Fan and Drum.

Their scheme was to link together their main forts, in this case Deva, now Chester, with Segontium, now Caernarfon. The field-fort of Canovium lay at the junction of this route with the way south, towards the other of the main Roman centres in Wales, Maridunum, which became Carmarthen. At Canovium on the Conwy river those roads joined, and the Segontium route set off across the hills along the ancient trackway, well into the margins of Snowdonia. Further south a similar approach took place from Carmarthen up past Dolgellau and along the road which became the A470, into the National Park towards Ffestiniog and Porthmadog.

This pattern, and particularly the easy access along the coast from Chester, has set the structure of the ways into Snowdonia, and hence brought about in history what we might now think of as the gateway towns. The northern route was followed by the Normans, under the influence of the Earls of Chester, the feudal marcher barons set up there precisely to promote the interests of the Norman kings. Like the Romans they invaded from their military base there. Unlike the Romans they came badly unstuck by overstretching their lines of supply. Briefly: because of the Welsh strategy of disappearing in front of the enemy and taking everything with them (then resorting to guerilla tactics from the mountains) there was no plunder to support the lines of advance in the rich lands lying between Chester and the Conwy river. Thus King Henry II, the first of the Plantagenet kings, was obliged to abort an invasion, caught in bad weather on the Berwyn mountains, because of that and 'lack of food', in 1165. In 1211 King John tried invasion again, and the army gathered at Chester. Across evacuated land they came unhindered to Deganwy, while the people of northern Wales under their Llywelyn Fawr ('the Great') waited in the mountains across the river. There at Deganwy the invaders starved, ending by eating their horses.

The Romans had not relied on what became the medieval assumption of requisition, and supplied their army by sea at the other end. But now the Welsh controlled the coast and the river harbours, and later desperate attempts to feed besieged troops at Deganwy failed.

When King John tried again he had learnt from this bitter lesson. He came, well provisioned, from the south, from Oswestry across to the river Conwy in its higher reaches – meaning that something approximate to the route of the A5 already existed. There it was easier to deal with the barrier of the Conwy, and part of his army penetrated to Bangor, presumably through the mountains.

Two wings of approach to Snowdonia were thus well established early, and it is these which lay before Thomas Telford when he was commissioned to improve the roads of Britain for the new wave of faster travel, itself one of the seminal innovations of our history.

Coaching routes had become established throughout Britain before the 18th century. The first road map was produced to illustrate this by John Ogilby in 1675. He shows the mail-coach line from London as running up through Chester and thence by Denbigh and the eastern uplands (the coast being then largely marsh) to reach the Conwy river at what is now Glan Conwy Corner. In other words, it was neither the road taken by the kings and the earls of Chester, which we know went further north, by Flint and Rhuddlan, nor that used by King John along the Dee valley. This old coaching route, 'the Great Irish Road', fell out of use after Telford's definitive revision, and is now a series of rural lanes.

By the end of the 18th century there was a coaching road in use between Llangollen and the Conwy valley, the mail-coach route via Shrewsbury being for a time a rival to that by Chester. One more factor helped to set the pattern which presented itself to Telford. The quarrying of slate which started to become industrial in the 18th century led to the first tentative roads within the mountain area, and Lord Penrhyn's road of 1791 through Nant Ffrancon to serve his quarries was extended, as a turnpike trust, all the way to Capel Curig and then through Betws-y-coed to Pentrefoelas, in 1802.

At that time Telford was working on civil engineering projects in Scotland, but he was already familiar with the borders of northern Wales through having been appointed (in 1787) surveyor of public works in Shropshire, and between 1793 and 1805 he worked on the Ellesmere canal, constructing among other things the remarkable Pont Cysyllte aqueduct. When in 1810 a House of Commons committee was required to determine the future of the road through Wales to Ireland it was hardly surprising that they appointed Telford to survey and report.

Telford's main influence on our subject was his decision to accept the reality of the combination of the new turnpike trust with the old coaching route to instigate a national road through the heart of Snowdonia, inevitably bringing Betws-y-coed into prominence in the process. Later work which he undertook on the route from Chester also brought the Conwy crossing and hence the old town of Conwy into the new network of travel.

The gateways

The gateway towns to Snowdonia are thus of several sorts. There are the military towns, such as the old administrative centre Caernarfon, built on the basis of the Roman infrastructure which skirted the highland massif, later becoming the seat of a Norman outpost and then used by Edward I as part of the chain enclosing Gwynedd; and that of Conwy which was rather more purpose-built by Edward. There are the market and production towns, sited at the interface of the block with the more populated world, in this case exemplified by Dolgellau, lying just on the border of the National Park and at the head of a major route to the world to the south beyond. And there are towns which are (now) and originally were specifically posting points, of which Betws-y-coed is a prime example, and Porthmadog, built as an export harbour and now (as a result of its history) the focus of northern Wales's special contribution to communication, the narrow-gauge railways.

If we take these five towns in their three categories as typifying gateways it is with the recognition that others might have joined them. But some of the towns on the tourist routes are too distant from Snowdonia to be gateways to it, and form (like Llangollen or Denbigh) more of a gateway to north Wales in general. They (and others in our area, such as Bangor and Blaenau Ffestiniog) will be dealt with elsewhere, in relation to other aspects of their character. Here we are concerned with a consideration of what it is to be on the edge of something of such strong identity, and to be in the business of offering a way in.

II   The Gateway Towns

Conwy

There are a number of precedents for the town of Conwy. It is essentially the fortified protection of a river crossing. Its immediate predecessor lies across the river, within sight, where the hill above Deganwy, the Vardre, rises significantly above the estuary. There indeed the fort which protected the harbour and the coastline was in existence in the dark ages, and remained in place until the 13th century. Supposedly the seat of Maelgwn, king of Gwynedd, who died in 547, Deganwy castle was destroyed and rebuilt alternately by the Earls of Chester and the Princes of Wales, until in 1277 Edward I decided not to continue this long tradition, but to possess the river crossing first and then defend it on the enemy bank.

Edward had looked across the river from Deganwy when he visited what was by then his castle in 1256, before he became king, coming from Chester as, now, earl of that town – a title borne still by the heir to the throne. He seems to have been a natural strategist, and he spotted a principle which the Romans before him had grasped: you do not defend a river crossing from the wrong side of the river, when the enemy holds the further bank and can curtail your movements and prevent your supplies from reaching you. His father, Henry III, and his grandfather King John had both

Conwy's predecessor, a fort overlooking the river at Deganwy, stood on the hill known as the Vardre

Llywelyn the Great gave a charter to the monastery which occupied the area of Conwy, and his statue stands in the town's square as its founder

encountered this mistake at Deganwy. Probably none of them knew of the nearby example of the Roman fort at Caer Rhun, one of Conwy's other precedents, where the little garrison fort which held the crossing lay on the western bank. Presumably neither they nor the Romans took account of the other example, another precedent for Conwy, The Iron Age hillfort on the summit of Conwy mountain, just west of the present town, overlooking the river mouth and the bay.

Both the hillfort and the Roman camp illustrate a principle which Edward followed, presumably (since we cannot think he had time or materials to study history) instinctively. They are part of a chain or network, in which each example lies within reach of the next. Conwy should not be seen then, in its origins, as on its own: Edward had in mind from the start a chain of castle-towns encircling Gwynedd. This historic fact is recognized now by the designation of the World Heritage Site of which Conwy forms a part, since it and Caernarfon, Harlech and Beaumaris are not Heritage Sites on their own, but all are part of one, the Welsh castles of Edward I.

The situation which happened here was the culmination of a long and bitter period of history. Before the Norman Conquest the kingdoms which formed Wales were variously in alliance and dispute with the kingdoms which only gradually cohered to form England, those of the Angles of Mercia and Northumberland and the Saxons of Wessex. It was the arrival of the Normans in Chester and Shrewsbury which set up what became a traditional hostility.

Gwynedd and Powys began to experience the sharp edge of the feudal system. By that system of government men such as Hugh d'Avranches, first earl of Chester, and Roger of Montgomery at Shrewsbury, whose families had been brought with the king from France for the purpose and who notably kept the names of their French territories, were placed on the kingdom's borders (beyond which were dragons and savages) because they were powerful and ruthless, committed no doubt to the less than delicate principle that might is right. In exchange for the duty of preventing loss of territory they had a certain leeway in the opposite direction, and could, in effect, acquire what they could grab. This had the advantage that the king could largely forget about his borders, and it only had the snag, it appears, that when these henchmen got themselves into trouble he had to come and help them sort it out. This is partly why three kings in a row had to march from London to come to the aid of the earls of Chester.

When Llywelyn ap Gruffydd pulled down Deganwy castle in 1263, because it had proved too useful to the invading forces, the event became part of the sequence which led to war and finally conquest by Edward.

Seeing Conwy as primarily the garrison town which Edward built, we might ignore the fact that there was a settlement here before. When we first hear of it, in the Itinerary of Giraldus Cambrensis (recording his journey through Wales in 1188 with Archbishop Baldwin) Gerald mentions that he crossed the river downstream of '*the Cistercian monastery of Conwy*'. This abbey we know was given its charter by Llywelyn the Great in 1189, but was evidently already in existence a few years prior to that. Later the monastery, originally seeking peace and seclusion in this idyllic place, came into unfortunate contact with the greater world, when, in 1245, Henry III's army, stuck at Deganwy, sent a body of men across the river into the enemy area. Evidently equating the Cistercians with the hostile Welsh they sacked the Abbey:

> Our people then returned ... And, like greedy and needy men, indulged in plunder, and spread fire and rapine through the country on the other side of the water, and, among other profane proceedings, they irreverently pillaged a convent of the Cistercians, called Aberconway, of all its property, and even of the chalices and books, and burnt the buildings belonging to it.

When he decided to build Conwy as a castle-town Edward moved the monks. Clearly it would suit neither him nor them to have a religious house in the middle of a fortified colony. He sought the consent of the Pope, and a Papal Bull explained to the monks that '*your Monastery for many reasonable causes could not remain conveniently in the place where it then was*'. The Abbey was removed wholesale up the Conwy river to Maenan, mollified by the gift of rights and privileges, such as exemption from taxes and tolls. The Abbey church became the Parish church of the new town, which thus provides the only certain visible contact with the ancient monastery today.

We may assume this great Abbey to have existed around its church, and so to have been conclusively levelled in the process of laying out the grid-pattern of the medieval town. Foundations of it perhaps lie under the shops on High Street. One building here today perhaps incorporates its stone work. When Conwy burnt, as it did in several times of turmoil, all its wooden buildings were destroyed, with the result that we have now only one house left from its medieval period: Aberconwy House, at the corner of High Street and Castle Street, the base of which, unusually for the time, was made of stone. Perhaps we can see in this the fine and substantial stonework which the Cistercians used for the more important of their buildings.

The church itself has been considerably altered over the centuries, and only certain pieces of it are the work of the monks, identifiable mainly at its western end. The Cistercians did not have towers on their churches, so the western end of their Abbey church ends above the lancet windows where a break in the stonework can be seen. Those windows themselves, and the fine Early English doorway are their work, and so a hundred years older than the castle.

Llywelyn the Great, who gave the monks their charter, evidently took a close personal interest in Conwy, and in the end was buried there. The monks took his sarcophagus with them to Maenan, where its whereabouts became forgotten, the whole matter being disrupted by the Dissolution of the Monasteries, and a long time later the base of the stone casing turned up again and is today in the Wynn chapel at Llanrwst

The lancet windows of the west front and its door are almost all that remain of the original abbey church

Edward incorporated Llywelyn's hall into his town wall, resulting in the unusual feature of windows in its battlements

church. Llywelyn's final burial place is not known. In Conwy one more memory of him still exists, since he built for himself a fine hall there which Edward incorporated into his new town wall. This decision, which seems to have been an act of respect, has the unusual consequence that the town wall has windows in the outside at this point. The statue of Llywelyn in the square, given to the town by Albert Wood, the owner of Bodlondeb, rightly recognises him rather than Edward as Conwy's founder.

Although Conwy castle has royal apartments, this is more a matter of conventional design than an indication of its use. The local story of Edward's queen growing flowers on the east barbican, though appealing, is fantasy. Queen Eleanor came here once with the king when heavily pregnant, in the spring of 1284, probably briefly on the way to Caernarfon, where they camped for some time while she gave birth. Far from its being something of a family home, Edward himself only visited Conwy on one other occasion, after the death of his queen and in rather less fortunate circumstances. In the winter of 1294 and for the first week of 1295 he was stuck there, during the time of the rebellion of Madog ap Llywelyn, having lost his baggage train in an ambush near Bangor and being cut off from his supply lines by the flooded Conwy river. Notably the castle was in such short supply of food and wine that they had to postpone Christmas, which they celebrated when the river abated and provisions could arrive from Chester.

Conwy walled town was built by Edward as part of a plan to stabilise Wales by imposing on it a neat system of administration, set out in the Statute of Rhuddlan of 1284. This, roughly the county system of local government which has persisted ever since, required the presence of state officials in a network through the conquered country. The idea was that Norman colonists would be tempted to occupy the castle towns by the offer of property and privileges. The fact that Conwy remained largely empty for some time indicates that it didn't work. Being given the rights of burgage was not sufficient temptation to settle in these remote places, surrounded by hostile foreigners. Nevertheless the town remained for a long time defiantly English, and the Welsh, who naturally came from the surrounding country to trade during the day, were excluded after curfew, when the bell was rung and the gates closed. Tradition says that the hole in the wall at the end of Pool Lane, opening on to Mount Pleasant, was where they then came back in.

Conwy's identity as a stronghold brought it several times into history. Two of its major events took place within a few years of each other at the turn of the 14th to the 15th centuries. Once again a king came to Conwy, and once again not in favourable circumstances. Richard II was away in Ireland for a crucial period when his rival, the exiled Henry Bolingbroke, landed in Yorkshire and made his way to Chester to confront the king on his return. Richard was delayed in Ireland by the weather, but was confident on his return that he would be supported by a Welsh army, which he awaited first at Caernarfon, then at Conwy. The army, which had indeed been there, had dispersed during his delay, since the

The 'hole in the wall' in Pool Lane is said to be the way the local people came back into town after curfew

The Earl of Northumberland swore safe-conduct to Richard II in the chapel of Conwy Castle as a way of enticing him out

rumour had been spread that he was dead. Richard thus found himself in Conwy castle with only a handful of followers.

Henry had advanced to Flint, and sent his henchman the Earl of Northumberland to try to tempt the king out of the impregnable walls of Conwy. Negotiations continued for some days, in August 1399, between the two distrustful parties. Finally Richard agreed to go to meet Bolingbroke at Flint, and Northumberland guaranteed him safe conduct, convincing the suspicious king by swearing an oath on the 'Body of Our Lord', after the two of them had heard mass, in the chapel of Conwy castle.

It was a trick and a trap, since the earl had left a substantial army behind the headland of Penmaenrhos, that massive outcrop just the other side of Colwyn Bay. The king and his small band of supporters rode innocently into capture by them, hemmed in by the sea and the rock. It was the culmination of an act of deceit and blasphemy which still has the power to shock.

Richard's fall to Bolingbroke, of which this is the first movement, led to a period of unrest in Wales which provided the setting for the country's major uprising. Richard had been a popular king with the Welsh, who possibly believed the rumours that he was still alive. When (through several slight and in themselves not compelling disagreements) Owain Glyndŵr became a proclaimed enemy of the king, Wales exuberantly rose in rebellion under him, and for a time it seemed likely that a long-awaited independence would be achieved. Conwy found itself, in 1401, thrust into a central role in this story.

The family of Tudor of Penmynydd in Anglesey, more correctly written at the time as Tudur, was already an old-established one in Welsh terms, well-connected landowners with some considerable local influence. They were cousins of Owain Glyndŵr's and so naturally figured among his most prominent supporters in the north. Henry came in person with his army to Bangor and Caernarfon to deliver a hint which was widely taken up: much of the power of northern Wales submitted to him – but not the Tudors. When, in 1401, Henry pardoned all those who had done the practical thing and changed sides he explicitly excluded Owain himself and his Tudor cousins.

It was an early Easter in 1401, Good Friday falling on April 1st, and it is to be assumed that Conwy was full during the day that weekend of people from the country round about. The Tudor brothers, Rhys and Gwilym, were among them, with some forty friends. When the garrison of the castle came down to hear mass in the Parish church they forced their way into the castle without much problem. It was the only time that the castle fell to assault, and once inside it the Tudors found themselves impregnable within its highly sophisticated defences. The Welsh from the country around were quick to take their opportunity and occupy, and largely burn, the town. It was only regained for the crown by negotiation, and by late June the Tudors had the pardon which had been withheld, and left Conwy free men.

By the next time the defences of Conwy came under assault this medieval armoury was plainly out of date. The Parliamentary army, encamped in the Gyffin valley,

Vertical lines around the doorway of Conwy church are the results of soldiers superstitiously sharpening their arrows there

Contrasting styles of domestic architecture record the separate periods of Conwy's expansion

bombarded the walls from several directions with canon fire. The people of Conwy were afraid that it would be destroyed, and with the intervention of the Archbishop of York, John Williams, a Conwy man who had taken refuge there in the troubled times, the town fell to the Parliamentarians. That was in August, 1646, but still the Royalist garrison in the castle could not be shifted, and only when they surrendered due to shortage of provisions was the castle taken, in that November. That was its last use as a military provision.

During these times of conflict no doubt Conwy lived with a sense of danger. Nervous soldiers in its streets seasoned the daily lives of its merchants and tradespeople. Some physical evidence of the effects of war on Conwy remains, since the sandstone uprights around the church door bear the incisions of arrow-sharpening there. We do not know when or under what circumstances, but we may reasonably guess at a superstition by which your arrows gained better power if you sharpened them on a church doorway.

During the Middle Ages the town developed within its walls into a self-consciously English colony. The burgesses demanded of the king that

Welshmen shall purchase no land within the English town or franchise of the same ... Also, that the porter of Conwey, which is now a Welshman, may be put out, and the office given to an English Burgess inhabiting in the said town ... for it is no more meet for a Welshman to bear any office in Wales, or especially in any of the three English towns, than it is for a Frenchman to be officer in Calais, or a Scot in Berwick.

It was, by necessity, a trading town, and based on the river, where from the start (from the days of Giraldus) ferries had crossed, both at the Deganwy narrows and to the castle rock. It is from these roots that its identity grew, firstly as a posting point when travel became more frequent and with more commercial value, in the 17th and then, primarily the 18th centuries; then as an exporting port, after the problem of its river crossing had been solved.

The present physical makeup of the town reflects these two periods of success. During the late 18th century, when the mail coach came this way and larger numbers of self-important passengers, Conwy cashed in by housing them as they waited for the ferry, which was governed by weather and tides. We can still see the courtyards of coaching inns patterning the town layout. The rows of decidedly modest cottages of this time testify to the presence of a workforce to service this industry. They sit alongside (as in Rosemary Lane) much grander residences of Conwy's next expansion, after Telford had built the causeway and the bridge and Conwy could ship goods from the river's eastern side, and consequently the Quay was built, in 1833, and Conwy became for the time being an important port.

There is evidence that notable travellers came this way, as they must, on the road to Ireland during these two centuries. Daniel Defoe crossed here in 1725, Samuel Johnson, with his friends the Thrales, in 1774. In

1854 Charlotte Bronte and her new husband broke their journey here for a couple of days on their way to complete their honeymoon in Ireland. They arrived in Conwy the day of the wedding, and it was not a very hopeful start. Charlotte had a cold, and the weather was *'wet and wild'*. *'However'* (she wrote to her friend Ellen Nussey) *'we are sheltered in a comfortable inn'*, which is generally assumed to have been the Castle Hotel.

One person who did not come to Conwy, as far as we know, is William Wordsworth; and it is clear that the grave marked *'We Are Seven'* in the churchyard is entirely spurious. As it happens most people do not know of his poem of that name anyway, so are merely mildly puzzled by it as they pass. It is, it must be said, a dreadful poem, mawkish, trivial, repetitive, and written in a kind of jingling doggerel, in which the poet meets a little girl in a churchyard who insists that her family consists of seven people, in spite of the fact that some of them are buried nearby. Wordsworth used the place-name Conway, presumably because it scanned:

> *And two of us at Conway dwell,*
> *And two are gone to sea.*

Conwy has enough authentic links with the past not to need a fake one, and it is time to clear this matter up. I quote from the notes in de Selincourt's definitive edition. He in turn quotes Wordsworth:

Written at Alfoxden in the spring of 1798, under circumstances somewhat remarkable. The little girl

31

Thomas Telford redesigned the road layout through Conwy and in the process built the Bangor arch

Reliable documentary evidence shows the supposed source of Wordsworth's poem 'We Are Seven' to be entirely spurious

who is the heroine I met within the area of Goodrich Castle in the year 1793.

He and his sister and Coleridge set off from Alfoxden to walk through the Quantocks to Watchet and Linton, and on the way planned 'The Poem of the Ancient Mariner', and when they came back to Alfoxden they found they had not achieved what they intended, which was to produce some poetry to be sold to the New Monthly Magazine to pay for their holiday. The Ancient Mariner had expanded by then to be too great a project to serve this purpose. '*Accordingly I wrote The Idiot Boy, Her eyes are wild, etc., We are seven, The Thorn, and some others.*'

> To return to We are seven, the piece that called forth this note, I composed it while walking in the grove at Alfoxden. My friends will not deem it too trifling to relate that while walking to and fro I composed the last stanza first, having begun with the last line.

Alfoxden is a property in Somerset, near Holford, which the Wordsworths had rented for a long period in 1797, in order to spend some time with Coleridge, who was living nearby. Goodrich Castle, where Wordsworth had met the little girl five years earlier, stands above the river Wye not far from Monmouth. Later in their 1798 tour they again went up the Wye, '*and so on to N. Wales, to the Vale of Clwyd, where I spent my summer under the roof of the father of my friend, Robert Jones*'. Had he come to Conwy it seems likely he would have said so.

It is often said that Conwy is unaltered from the town plan which Edward laid out, and its walls still complete, but in fact Thomas Telford carried out considerable modifications of the old town and destroyed large sections of it, in the process of directing the main road traffic through its streets and thus giving rise to a traffic problem which was not to be solved for a further hundred and seventy years. He breached the walls in Castle Square, cut a swathe through the town's buildings up through what is now Rosehill Street, opened up the square and ploughed another hole in the wall where a drum tower was converted to be the Bangor Arch. To get some feeling of what the medieval town was like you have to imagine coming into town by Church Street, which led you directly into the market square, then enclosed at the town's heart.

Conwy is a posting point again now, being a convenient base from which to visit Anglesey and the National Park. Although its several historical roles have been superseded, it still bears the physical form of a river-crossing point, of the setting-off port for the bay and the ocean, and with its surviving mussel-fishing industry a firm reminder of its more recent character as a fishing port. The boastful fortress on the rock and the encircling wall reinforce physically the town's dominant social attitude, which is a stalwart sense of identity, the feeling which the small community has of belonging to a recognizable place.

Caernarfon

The Roman fort Segontium looks out from its elevated position across the level land to the peak of Tre'r Ceiri, site of one of Britain's major hillforts. In the same way Viroconium, at Wroxeter, looks towards the great iron-age fortress on the Wrekin, and this form has numerous other instances in south Wales and southern England, so that we may suppose that this geographical confrontation was a symptom of a policy decision, to keep those settlements which were not to be destroyed under observation and in check. The strength of Segontium allowed Tre'r Ceiri to continue to be occupied, and indeed, we may guess from its periods of use, to become the haven for refugees from *pax romana* in a wider area – and thus, ironically, to provide a link for Wales with its pre-Roman independence.

Quite early on, when Roman policy had moved from retaliation to containment and Segontium had become a major feature of the encirclement of the mountainous area by military forts and the penetration of it by the great roads which linked them to the national network of the ordered colony, some people at least came down from Tre'r Ceiri and (as all over the Empire) allowed themselves to be romanised. When it was the home of the 20th Augustan Legion, Segontium was accompanied by an extensive civil town outside the fort's defences, in connection with which have been found a Mithraic temple and a cemetery. The parish church of Caernarfon, (St Peblig's, from Publicius, supposed son of the Roman Emperor Magnus Maximus), is an emblem

*The Roman town of Segontium, Caernarfon's predecessor,
lies just outside and above it*

The Parish Church, St Peblig's, lies just outside the Roman fort

of the fact of the town's having started here, with the offshoot of an enemy fort, since the church lies just outside the Roman fort and in its walls was found a piece of Roman altar, probably from the ruins of the Mithraic temple destroyed on the rise of Christianity.

This uncharacteristic settlement, an early Welsh town, has now been largely built over and forgotten, but it accidentally set a precedent for Caernarfon's future, as a native offshoot from an outside military and administrative centre. When a future invader repeated the process, moving the whole thing downstream a little to the banks of the Seiont estuary, this pattern too was repeated.

Some time during the centuries between the sixth and fourteenth a folk-memory of early local history became elaborated into a national myth. Gildas in the mid sixth century and the authors of the *Historia Brittonum* of about 830 recognised that the Roman withdrawal from Britain was a significant event, the effects of which were felt in Wales.

The tale of *Macsen* which eventually resulted, known to us from manuscripts of the 14th century, tells the tale from the native point of view, imagining the fantasy of Welsh responsibility for Roman achievement.

Macsen, already Emperor of Rome, came to Britain (it says), and specifically to Caernarfon, as the result of a dream, in which he fell in love with the princess of that area. She is identified in the story as Elen Luyddog, 'Elen of the Hosts', an ancestral mythic figure said to be the daughter of Eudaf, a local chieftain who supposedly held Segontium for the Romans; and it is said in the tales that later, married to the Emperor, she was responsible for the founding of the Roman towns, still known as such in the early middle ages, such as Caerleon and Carmarthen, and for having the roads built which were such a prominent feature in early times, when otherwise only horse tracks linked the settlements. Hence the designation of the Roman road here, part of a route which runs through Wales, as Sarn Helen, Helen's causeway. There are several errors of history here, since a confusion arose between this Elen and St Helena, the mother of Constantine the Great who was credited with discovering in Jerusalem the True Cross. The latter, however, was a generation older than the wife of Macsen would have been, and in any case never came to Britain. Moreover it is possible that the name of this road, and of others which are also known as Sarn Helen, derives not from an Empress at all but from the Welsh word *elin*, which means the forearm between wrist and elbow, which suggests that they were straighter roads than previous primitive paths.

In the story Macsen leaves Caernarfon with his army to confront the alternative emperor in France, and this theme too is paralleled in history, since there was a massive withdrawal of the legions in the 4th century. Archaeology shows that Segontium was also largely evacuated at that time, only a small garrison remaining for a few years after 383, the year of Maximus's invasion of Gaul. The story says that the Welsh troops he took ('Elen's brothers') stayed in continental Europe, and even invaded Rome.

A further odd footnote to this story arose from the discovery of a mention in the *Notitia Dignitatum* (a sort

The remains of the Norman motte can still be seen under the Queen's Tower

The town on the 'Welsh' side of the river Cadnant rises in a piecemeal fashion in contrast to the formal grid formation of the walled town

of gazetteer) of 429 AD, of a legion known as the Segontientes, serving in the Balkans.

Segontium itself was not on the banks of the river Seiont, as is shown by the fact that the Romans also had a port here which was. That is now, like so much in this area, partly under modern buildings. The portions of wall which remain. *Hen Waliau*, are possibly part of a later fort connected with the port; they stand now above the main road in people's gardens, fine specimens of Roman walling still rising to near their original height.

Maybe the Seiont silted or the land around its mouth extended, because the next invader to build a fortress here did so downstream, setting the pattern for a wholesale shift of the town in that direction. Hugh Lupus, Earl of Chester, also known as Hugh d'Avranches (after his home town in France), had been granted land on the Welsh border by William the Conqueror in 1067, and in the reign of the Conqueror's son William Rufus he extended his mandate far west into Wales, building castles at Deganwy and Aber Lleiniog in Anglesey, and also here at Caernarfon, probably about 1090. The expansion was overconfident and it did not last, but the basis of his castles did, the huge motte which is such an effective military tool. Hugh's mound at Caernarfon was still there when King Edward came, and indeed (as he did with Llywelyn's hall at Conwy) the great castle-builder incorporated it into his new scheme. It was still prominent here in fact as late as about 1870, and indeed it is still actually there and discernible in the bank under the Queen's Tower, and explains the unexpected height of the Queen's Gate and also the difference in level

The name 'Mill Lane' is the only sign now of the mills around the river Cadnant

The river Cadnant, which once acted as a moat between the walled town and the Welsh settlement, is now invisible under a carpark

between the lower and the upper wards.

One effect of the elevation of the Queen's Gate, rearing over the Maes, or Castle Square, is that it invites ideas of proclamation, and it is here that a famous story envisages Edward presenting to the people of Wales his new-born son. Some facts as so often underlie this. Caernarfon was intended to become the seat of the ruler of northern Wales, a sort of Viceroy, but the Welsh (though apparently they to some extent trusted the king) were wary of being left under the rule of an English officer. In the event this scheme did not develop, and the castle here was never actually even finished; but there is enough inbuilt grandeur to demonstrate that the intention was that it should become the Viceroy's palace: the Roman references, for instance, in the specific imitation of Constantinople by the decorative banding in the stonework, making Caernarfon the successor to that eastern imperial city, itself called after the supposed son (by a confusion of Helens) of Macsen of Segontium. Roman eagles were to decorate the towers, and indeed the remnants of one still testifies to this on the Eagle Tower. But no Viceroy emerged and this far western place gradually lost its relevance as a capital.

The story of the presentation of the infant prince is traceable to a book compiled by David Powel, a native of Denbighshire, *The Historie of Cambria, now called Wales*, published in 1584. Powel tells us that Edward could not bring the people of Wales 'to *yeeld their obedience to anie other Prince, except he were of their owne nation*'. The King sent for '*Queene Elianor out of England in the deepe of winter being then great with*

42

child, to the castell of Caernaruon' and when she had given birth he gathered the Welsh barons. He offered them *'one that was borne in Wales, and could speake neuer a word of English'* and *'when they all had granted that such a one they would obey, he named his owne sonne Edward borne in Caernaruon castell a few daies before'*. It is of course a favourite device of folktale, this trick by which someone is given what they ask for but not as they expect it.

Of course the fact that this tale cannot be found before the 16th century does not, by itself, mean that it is false. Powel was a meticulous scholar and at pains to convince his readers that he was not making anything up. In his introduction he gives more than twenty sources by name, and he largely followed the custom of giving marginal references of *'the page or chapters of the booke where thou shalt find the same historie treated of'*. Unfortunately he has not followed this helpful habit in these relevant paragraphs, so that all we have of provenance for this story is the imprecise prefix *'for the most part out of the records in the towre'*. The story's reliance on the mechanism of the folktale trick perhaps gives it away, but more I think the element of anachronism in the prominence of the language factor. After the Act of Union, in 1536, the Welsh were being actively encouraged to learn English in order to advance themselves. It is doubtful whether who spoke what would have been an issue in 1284. Edward himself, for instance, probably did not speak English. In any case English was a foreign language to him as well, the symbol of a conquered nation.

The idea that this supposed event was the first investiture of an English Prince of Wales, a fancy fostered by Lloyd George which conveniently resulted in giving his constituency, Caernarfon, and himself, the boost of some prominence, is also historically inept. Edward I did make his son Prince of Wales, and in so doing set the habit for all future monarchs; but he held the title vacant until, in 1301, it seemed to offer temptation for others to claim it. Edward of Caernarfon was sixteen when he was invested as Prince of Wales, at Lincoln.

The castle was envisaged as part of a walled complex occupying the whole of the headland between the Seiont and the Strait. Before the quay was built the south walls of the castle stood right on the water, and a water-gate was planned but never completed at the foot of the Eagle Tower. The town's main access was from the Menai Strait by the entrance known as Porth yr Aur, now home to the Royal Welsh Yacht Club. The form of the walled town can be seen quite clearly – though its wall is largely obscured by the town's buildings, by contrast with Conwy, where the walls visually overpower the town.

Outside the walled town on the landward side, where the Eastgate proclaims a clear distinction between inside and outside, lay the remains of the Welsh town which had been there before Edward came, and which was segregated in his plan not just by the building of the town wall but by the presence of the river Cadnant, which acted as a partial moat, running down through the Millpond, the 'Kings Pool', which occupied the area adjoining Castle Square. Pool Street, Pool Hill, and

Penllyn, notable now for a bus station and a multi-storey carpark, mark on the modern town this ancient feature. On the other side of Bridge Street (which crossed the end of the Pool) Mill Lane falls from Eastgate Street into a low lying area known as the Mill Lane dip, the site of the town's mills, and right underneath it, long ago vanished from sight but still there, is the river Cadnant, which flowed through the Pool from the meadows and valleys to the north-east, in the area of the village of Bethel, to emerge from Caernarfon into the Menai Strait near to what is now Bank Quay. Like so much around us, like the civil settlement at Segontium, like Hugh d'Avranche's motte, like the vast King's Pool, the Cadnant is so firmly submerged by subsequent Caernarfons that you would not know it was there or that it ever had been.

The fact of the mills and their associated waterpower being outside the walls, as indeed they were in Conwy, indicates that the relationship between the Welsh town and the English was one of co-operation rather than hostility. The river Cadnant did not in fact provide much of a barrier between the two, and it was from the outset bridged. The two towns appear to have had distinctly different characters, and indeed to a large extent they still do. The rigid grid pattern of the castle town, again an echo of its Roman predecessor, was alien to its Welsh neighbour. That scrambled rather haphazardly along its slope. This loose structure enables Caernarfon town today to turn its back physically on its famous asset, allowing few if any views of the magnificent monument from its commercial heart, for instance from Bridge

Street, or any way of knowing it was there until you actually turn into Y Maes and see, with some surprise, this huge cuckoo squatting in this modest nest.

Although its original intended role was as an administrative centre, both in its Roman and its Norman form, Caernarfon developed several layers of character not directly related to these roots. Its office as a centre of local government gave it a respectable status from the Middle Ages on, when the setting up in the borough of the king's exchequer in the relatively new county of Caernarfonshire brought into town officials, clerks and lawyers, whose presence as a feature of the place lent weight to its later traditional role as a legal centre. The exchequer was a sort of tax office, receiving from the sheriffs rents from towns and properties of which the crown was overall landlord within the county.

This superior role survived for some time. Sir John Wynn, of Gwydir, writing around the turn of the 16th to 17th centuries about his family history, remarked that '*In those days*' (the time his great-grandfather went to school) '*Caen'von flourished aswell by trade of merchandise as also for that the kings exchequer, Chauncerie and common lawe courts for all northwales was there contynuallie resideinge ...*' which he says made it also a centre of learning: '*wherebye civilitie and learninge flourished in that towne ...*' He had it on good authority, he says, that the records of the King's courts kept in Caernarfon in those days were as orderly and as well kept as those in Westminster. It was because his great-grandfather was sent to school there that he learnt to speak English and to write and understand Latin.

Although the influence of the exchequer declined in the 16th century, the presence of lawyers there on the king's business had established the town as a stronghold of law long before the magistrates courts started to hold sessions there in about 1536.

It is evident from Sir John's report that trading had also started to be a part of the town's activities, and by the end of the 18th century we find this to be well-established and in the process of being overlaid by a new industry, which we would now call tourism. When the Rev. Bingley came, in 1798, Caernarfon's historic habits were not forgotten: *'The court-house, in which the great sessions for the county are held, and where all the county business is done, stands nearly opposite to the castle gates ...'* Compared to this long tradition it seems the maritime function of the town was evidently then still relatively insignificant: *'there is a small, but tolerable good harbour'* which even by then was exporting *'many thousand tons'* of slates *'to different parts of the kingdom'*.

But it is Caernarfon's new role which strikes Bingley. He says it is *'the most beautiful town in North Wales'* and by the fortune of being set between the mountains and the island is *'a convenient place of residence for travellers who wish to visit both'*. As a result of this favourable position it had clearly become smart. A spacious room over one of the gates was used as a town hall *'in which the dancing assemblies are frequently held'* and the quay extended into a *'broad and pleasant terrace walk ... which is the fashionable promenade, on fine evenings, for all descriptions of people'*.

The splendidly pillared courthouse remains a physical monument to one strong line of Caernarfon's past, though the business of the county court has moved into sleek new buildings behind it. The slate quay (the older area of reclamation which lies between the castle and the river) is now largely a carpark. We have to remember that for an important period the life of the town faced this way. Competition between the quarry-owners increased with the start of the 19th century, by which time roofing-slates had become big business, and the makeup of the mountains lying above Bangor and Caernarfon had the same sort of effect on the area as coal had on south Wales. It was competition between the owners of the great quarry works of Dinorwig (Vaynol) and Bethesda (Penrhyn) which led to the building of a tramway down from the Nantlle valley to the slate quay at Caernarfon, in 1828. This was rather a late response – Lord Penrhyn had built Port Penrhyn and run a railway to it from his quarries in 1790 and 1801, and in any case Assheton Smith of Vaynol, whose family initially controlled Caernarfon, had already made the port here potentially redundant by the purpose-built exporting quays of Port Dinorwig and the tramway to it, in 1824. But the effect of building the slate quay in the first place had been to double Caernarfon's population, nearly five thousand people being added to it between the 1790s and the 1830s. The town spread then along the Seiont and inland it became more densely packed. Small houses crammed into groups around the upper side of Bridge Street became health-hazards, due to lack of running water and neglect of rubbish removal, and several epidemics of cholera broke out in the first half of the 19th century. Not much was done until one was so severe, in 1865, that a large area of insanitary housing was demolished and the town was then re-planned on a more open scheme. They had been warned. The Borough's own Grand Jury had announced in 1832 that

> owing to the rapid increase in number of inhabitants and the great influx of Visitors during the Summer months [nuisances] will if not timely abated present infectious diseases and cause strangers to abstain from making Caernarfon a place of Summer resort.

The town spread north towards Twthill, and by the end of that century it has become three times as large outside the walls as the old town within them. In the process a large area became redeveloped as the New Dock, and in the meantime (in 1852) the railway had arrived. A new sort of shipping trade developed.

The effect of the coming of the railway was that the focus of shipping became extended from the largely coastal trade in slates which had built up during the early 19th century. Welsh slates now went by sea to the USA and Canada, but by rail to Liverpool and Birmingham. Copper ore became an additional export, and timber, wines and spirits were imported, leading to the provision of bonded warehouses in the 1840s. This business was still based on the medieval slate quay, Cei Llechi, where the Harbour Trust had erected, in 1840, their fine headquarters building which still serves as the harbour office.

In the 1830s, however, the decision had been made to base Caernarfon's future on its seagoing trade, and the 'New Dock' was built by about 1830. This struggled to cope with expanding demand, not just in dock space but in related activities: ship-building and chandlery followed the increased need for shipping. By 1860 a larger dock space was evidently required urgently, and the decision was made to build the Victoria Dock, which was finished in 1874.

When the town turned towards the sea again in the 1830s its old streets were opened through the town wall onto Bank Quay in recognition of this new focus. We have to imagine a good deal of hubbub beyond the wall, where (according to J. Geraint Jenkins' book *Welsh Ships and Sailing Men*) 200 ships were built between 1758 and 1898. Now only the names of streets remain of that town of seafarers and adventurers, names referring to then contemporary history, 'The Turkey Shore', 'Balaclava Road', in a world which became subsequently preoccupied with carparks and flats. By then Caernarfon had for some time been engaged in the export of another commodity. Emigration to America became a trickle then a flood from the late 18th century, thousands of people leaving from the quays here during this time.

More recently Caernarfon has responded again with active involvement in the face of the results of hard times. By the mid 1980s over half the properties within the walled town were either derelict or at least vacant and for sale. An Independent Town Development Trust was formed in 1992 to tackle this problem and other cases of redundant buildings within the town. 'Galeri

The old Victoria Dock, once centre to Caernarfon's export shipping industry, is now reborn as an arts, leisure and residential complex

Caernarfon Cyf' takes the form of a limited company largely instigated by local businesses and community groups. It set about buying up and transforming Caernarfon's biggest eyesores, restoring buildings to a state in which they could be let. To date (2011) it has acquired, adapted and let over twenty-eight previously vacant properties. Its most ambitious and visible project is the revitalisation of the Victoria Dock itself, with the Galeri complex, a 'Creative Enterprise Centre' costing £7.5m, consisting of a 400 seat theatre-cum-cinema and various meeting rooms and exhibition areas, which opened on 7th March 2005.

Designed by the Liverpool architect Richard Murphy, this clean-cut, substantial building occupies one side of the Victoria Dock, facing onto the basin. It bears a practical rather than a decorative design, suitably slate-coloured in overall effect, even the wooden shuttering giving a stone-like appearance, the whole conveying a firm statement with an appropriate overall solidity. References to Caerarfon continue beyond the slate theme, with round stone wall-towers built into the façade of the neighbouring flats and hotel.

This magnificent enterprise testifies to Caernarfon's resilience. It provides an emblem now of what appears to be a long tradition, in that the place has always undergone periods of decline and then renewal.

Porthmadog

Porthmadog is rightly proud of its shops. They run unbroken for several hundred yards along its High Street, *Stryd Fawr*, giving the strong and not entirely misleading impression of a one-street, linear road-town. In summer they are cheerful and exuberant, busy with pavement displays and visual variety, awnings, open doors. In winter this is a grim scene, a reminder of the optimism of investing in a frail and seasonal market.

Shops though have nothing to do with Porthmadog's origins. Its development as a tourist town, and explicitly a gateway centre for the attractions of the National Park, which is its present successful character, is a symptom of the resilience and adaptability to change which such fundamentally accidental places cultivate within themselves. In theory Porthmadog should not really be there at all.

From very early times a large stretch of sand and salt-marsh had built up on the silt-plain which formed the tidal deltas of the rivers Glaslyn and Dwyryd, where they both sought the sea together, below, respectively, their sources in the Snowdon uplands and the Migneint watershed. This watery plain, known as Traeth Mawr and Traeth Bach, formed a barrier to communications, since a road heading south would have to deviate considerably before finding a fording place on the Dwyryd. And then come back down the other side. Those who wished to come this way did not, however, choose to go round, but waited for the tide and went straight across. Pennant, for instance, in the 18th century, referred to it as a '*most dangerous passage to strangers, by reason of the tides which flow here with great rapidity*', but he took that route all the same, of course with the security of a local guide. He was rewarded by '*the view from the middle of the sands towards Snowdonia*' which he said was '*most extravagantly wild*'.

That it was an old problem, with an old solution, is clear. In the Mabinogion tale of *Math son of Mathonwy* the warring armies of north and south Wales confronted each other at Dolbenmaen, where a battle took place resulting in a truce. The two sides came under truce to Traeth Mawr, but there fighting broke out again. Rather than subject everyone to another pitched battle it was decided that the two main protagonists should contest the matter in single combat – Gwydion and Pryderi, that is, the leaders of the rival powers of north and south Wales. They fought in that final duel on the tidal stretches, below the spectacular ranges. But it was not an equal combat. Gwydion was a great magician, and '*by force of power and craft, and magic and enchantment*' he prevailed, and Pryderi was killed. He was buried above Y Felenrhyd, and his grave (probably the ancient pillar in the wall of Maentwrog church) '*is still there*'.

It must be said that magic and enchantment does not always prevail like that, over physical might, and if they did perhaps the mountains which Pennant saw would still be mirrored in the high tides of the Traeth. There were, in the years which led the 19th century towards its great commercial achievements, powers at work through which commercial interests prevailed. It was on the back of that that Porthmadog fortuitously came into existence.

We need to see the thing briefly in the context of a wider world. It was not always certain that the main routes through northern Wales would follow the lines eventually chosen for them by the schemes of Thomas Telford. The route from London to Dublin became of increasing significance during the 18th century, and towards the beginning of the 19th it became obvious that a decision had to be made, and an official port established. What was not always obvious, however, was that the best way would be the traditional one, the ancient Roman route through Chester. The alternative road from London to Shrewsbury was just as much developed, and the route from there via Welshpool and Dolgellau offered several advantages. It avoided the problems of the crossings of the river Conwy and the Menai Strait, and it led to what would have been (it was thought) a better port than Holyhead: Porth Dinllaen, on the northern coast of Llŷn.

This is not as unrealistic as it now sounds. Porth Dinllaen then was a regular departure port for Ireland. For instance, in the first six months of the year 1804 alone 656 vessels had sailed to Ireland from there. It was (it must surprise us now to hear) a better port for this purpose than Holyhead. It had a permanent deep-water bay, whereas that of Holyhead was more tidally restricted and so led to the situation of vessels awaiting water for leaving harbour which could then miss the benefit of the tide in crossing the channel. For what seems to have been local political reasons Holyhead was chosen, however, and Porth Dinllaen now is a tiny peaceful village in its private arc of bay.

The whole thing must have seemed quite different when the Porth Dinllaen Harbour Company was formed in 1806, empowered to raise £12,000 to build a harbour which would rival Liverpool.

The only drawback at the time to this sound commercial scheme was the crossing of Traeth Mawr. For the road to have to rise from Dolgellau across the moors to Trawfynydd would have counteracted the project's natural advantages. The coastal route by Dyffryn Ardudwy and Harlech was much more tempting. But then there was, unavoidably, Traeth Mawr.

It was not initially with this matter in mind that William Alexander Madocks first started reclaiming the Traeth. His immediate concern was to increase, by reclamation, his personal land holding. During the Napoleonic wars the shortage of corn due to blockade had led to intensified agriculture in Britain and hence put up the price of land. The land which Madocks now owned at the edge of the Traeth was subject to flooding, making embankments anyway essential; but the silt-land beyond that was clearly fertile, once drained of its salt and free of its periodic inundation, and indeed it was only a few years before Madocks was growing oats on it.

As so often in his story greater circumstances overtook him. By the time he built Tremadog on his reclaimed land he clearly had the road from London to Dublin in mind. Tremadog was supposed to be on the new main road, a fact which is evidenced by the names of its streets: London Street met Dublin Street in its

The town of Tremadoc was built with the route from London to Ireland in mind

*The building of the embankment to reclaim Traeth Mawr
gave rise to a natural harbour which became Porthmadog*

central square. A coaching inn presides still over the quiet scene, quite out of proportion to the demands of the village now. Quite incidentally a part of this great enterprise then gave rise to Porthmadog.

To complete his scheme for the reclamation of the whole of the Traeth, Madocks gained an Act of Parliament in 1807 which permitted him to construct a one-and-a-half mile embankment, which in due course, with some set-backs and much expense, (and a whole set of involvements which are unfortunately not relevant here), put into Madocks's ownership the whole of the two Traeths. In the process it was apparently necessary to divert the river Glaslyn to run along the inside of the embankment and emerge through the new sluice gates at its western end. It was quite unexpected that in the process of doing so it would gouge out a deep pool at the point where it met the sea.

That unexpected basin became Porthmadog. The opportunity to construct a harbour there would not have been of such significance if there had not been an independent need for one. Madocks could not have foreseen this extra bit of luck. For quite some time the slate industry at Blaenau Ffestiniog had been expanding, with the demand for roofing slates brought about by the urbanisation of the late 18th century. It was a cumbersome and fragmented business. The slates came down by pack horse to be loaded onto barges at small quays (which may still be seen) on the river Dwyryd, and from there they were transferred to deep-water vessels beached on the sands, where the Dwyryd met the Glaslyn.

After the passing of a Parliamentary Bill work started on the new harbour in 1821. The same year Samuel Holland, then aged eighteen, arrived to take over the running of the Oakley quarries from his father. Holland injected a new professionalism into the business, and it was he who introduced, in the 1830s, a direct line by narrow-gauge railway from the quarry to the port.

At first this was a gravity-powered construction, the cars pulled back up by horses, which then rode back down in them with the slate. Holland and Porthmadog were, at the time, bang up to date, and steam was the new technology and the enabling force of the industrial age. Steam engines have operated on this line since October 1863.

Although the famous Ffestiniog narrow-gauge railway was a practical solution to a business-based problem, its recreational possibilities have been evident from the start. It began to carry passengers in 1865, and tourism became a large part of its support when the slate trade declined around 1900.

The much-loved railway is now staffed mainly by volunteers. Indeed it is to voluntary enthusiasts that it owes its current existence. The loss of the German market for roofing slates with the start of the first World War was further exacerbated by the loss of the tourist trade caused by the second. The railway closed completely in 1946, became overgrown and derelict, and was only resurrected by the enterprise of railway lovers in the 1950s. In phases during that decade they restored and repaired it and it reopened completely only in 1982, when a new station was constructed at Blaenau

Porthmadog's waterfront was once a busy industrial scene, of which there is now no sign

The three-masted schooners which were purpose-built for local conditions became famous sailing ships

Ffestiniog in conjunction with British Rail, not only to bring the 'little' railway right into the town but to link it with its larger colleague. It is now possible to do a railway circuit of Snowdonia, coming down the beautiful Conwy Valley line to Llandudno-Junction and going on from there to Bangor.

Porthmadog as a port was already in existence before the coming of the railway, but its phenomenal rise to prosperity was fuelled by that and by the enterprise of Samuel Holland. The population of Porthmadog in 1821, when Holland came, was 885. By 1861 it was over three thousand. It doubled between 1851 and 1881. As elsewhere such hasty expansion led to problems, slum conditions arising in overcrowded developments, and epidemic resulting in the 1850s. The old track across the now reclaimed land was straightened and became Stryd Fawr, the present High Street.

This was all on the back of a fast expanding trade in slate, led at first by the German market. Even today, in spite of time and blitzing, much of Hamburg is roofed with Ffestiniog slates, which all left from the quays of Porthmadog. The price of slate had doubled between 1798 and 1825, in which year Ffestiniog produced 10,000 tons, though still pre-railway and so all horse-drawn. By 1873 more than 116,000 tons of slates were exported from here in more than a thousand ships.

Coal, lime and timber were brought in. Also inevitably quantities of ballast were required, to bring home empty the essentially light and shallow-drafted boats, and this has found its way into the walls of some of Porthmadog's houses. The island in the Glaslyn which one sees looking out to sea from the old wharfs is still called Cei Ballast, the ballast quay, or the wall of ballast.

Besides the export of slate to the developing British towns and those of Germany Ffestiniog slates went from here to Liverpool for onward export to Australia, and later went direct to Newfoundland and Labrador. This required a very special sort of boat, and by a process of evolution there came into being the iconic Porthmadog schooner, known as the Western Ocean Yacht.

It was necessary for these sailing ships to weigh less than two hundred tons, in order to avoid the requirement of the Merchant Shipping Act that ships of more than that must have a licensed mate. The crew of seven or eight were local people whose background was the land, and they adapted themselves to these long voyages with more tenacity than technology.

> Great in this
> They made small ships do
> Big things, leaping hurdles
> Of the stiff sea, horse against horses
> In the tide race.

So R. S. Thomas describes them, in his poem *Schoonermen*.

More than two hundred of these tough little ships were built at Porthmadog, between 1891 (when the *Blodwen* was launched) and 1913, when the last of them, the *Gestiana* left the slipway.

The boats were also suited to another purpose, which supplemented their business on the coast of Canada.

The much-loved railways centred on Porthmadog are an essential element of its history and of its present popularity

Porthmadog's past as a quarry outlet is still visible in its impressive stone buildings

They carried out a service to the fishing trade, bearing salt from Europe to Canada for salting cod, and carrying salted cod back again to pass on to ports in the Mediterranean.

They were three-masted sailing ships with fore-and-aft sails, which allowed them to beat to windward with short tacks off this habitually lee shore with a strong landward drift and the tendency to sudden build-up of short waves, a progress which would have been hard and hazardous for squatter vessels. It is hard to imagine now, looking at the flat banks in the estuary and the bay, often deceptively peaceful in the calm of a summer day, how this complex shore can change and deceive. Circumstances imposed on the population of the lower Ffestiniog valley a maritime heritage which the land itself shows no sign of offering.

> From long years
> In a salt school, caned by brine,
> They came landward
> With the eyes of boys,
> The Welsh accent
> Thick in their sails.

The town too, as well as its foreshore, adapted itself to its primary role, now largely only a memory. Pencei, for instance, an area now not much used except for a pub, a seating area and a carpark, was a hubbub of boat-building and servicing, slate loading and trading. Only the sturdy architecture of the old buildings there still being brought into re-use, reminds us of the connection

Conwy

Conwy castle from the south side

*The view from the top tower of the town wall shows the compact form
of the town within the walls*

Llywelyn ap Iorwerth was the original founder of Conwy

Plas Mawr, in the High Street, is a rare example of an Elizabethan town house

Conwy has always been closely connected with the business of fishing

Long before the town of Conwy was built a hillfort served the same purpose of defending the river access

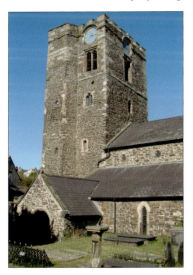

The Parish church is based on the abbey church of the Cistercian monastery

Conwy's medieval street fairs are still continued

Stephenson's tubular railway bridge is less architecturally refined than Telford's elegant suspension bridge

Caernarfon

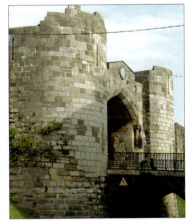

The castle looms above the town and the old town within the walls is still a separate area in contrast to Caernarfon's organic growth

Owain Glyndŵr's attack on the colony is commemorated on Twtil

A tribute to another Welsh prince – Llywelyn II

The courthouse with its fine portico lies directly opposite the castle

The parlour office occupies the headquarters of the Harbour Trust erected in 1840

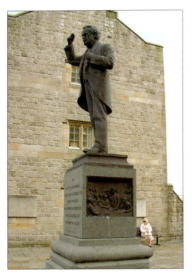

The prominent statue of Lloyd George bears a memory of the town's modern importance

Porth yr Aur, originally the main access to the town from the Menai Strait

Porthmadog

The embankment which protected the reclaimed land of Traeth Mawr also gave rise inadvertently to Porthmadog

Porthmadog's main feature is its fine line of shops

The harbour once busy with slate exporting is now entirely recreational

Dolgellau

The old Llanelltyd bridge over Mawddach river, near Dolgellau

Below Dolgellau, on the Mawddach, are many scenic spots, such as Penmaenpool

Traditional architecture in the heritage centre of Dolgellau

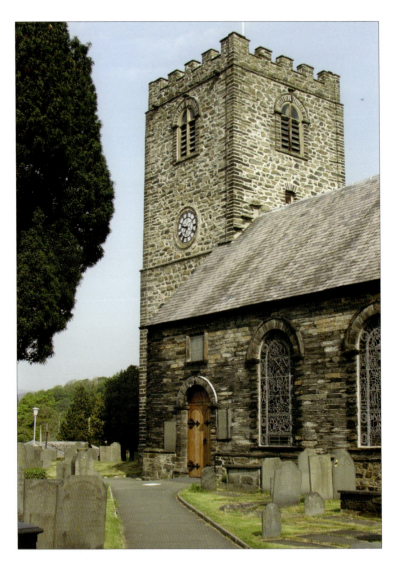

The church of Dolgellau dates mainly from the 18th century

The old Roman Road, Sarn Elen, above Betws-y-coed

Tŷ Hyll, on the Capel road above Betws,
is a fine example of locally stone-built dwellings

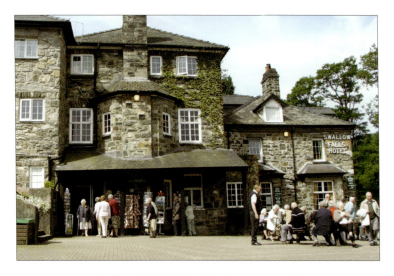

Swallow Falls Hotel and the famous waterfall

The fifteenth century stone bridge, Pont-y-pair

St Mary's church, Betws-y-coed

The old church of St Michael's,
Betws-y-coed

The historic route of
Thomas Telford's A5,
which runs through the village

Llyn Elsi above Betws-y-coed

with the Oakley quarries.

Much of Porthmadog's first function, that of supplying the construction of British cities, was taken away from it when the Cambrian Railway opened in 1867. Its future turns out to have remained railroad-based, however, and the recent revival of the Welsh Highland Railway gives yet another dimension to its role as gateway.

The Welsh Highland Railway sprang in part from a track built to take slate down from the Croesor quarries to Porthmadog in the 1860s. The lower bit of this, the Croesor tramway, was eventually joined up with a stretch which had initiated the tunnels through the Aberglaslyn Pass, the '*Portmadoc, Beddgelert and South Snowdon Railway*', and another stretch developed to Rhyd Ddu and Bryngwyn in the 1880s. Through a merger of companies the Welsh Highland Railway Society which became WHR Ltd. was in due course formed from a base starting in 1922. After showing initial promise with a successful year in 1923 it proved uncommercial. There was no freight trade, since the slate industry had already declined, and passenger service could not compete, in days before the development of tourism, with the local bus. The company was forced into receivership by the area's council in 1927, and in due course, in 1933, it closed. The next year it was leased by the receivers to the Ffestiniog Railway company, but the tourist trade remained insufficient to serve both railways, and it failed again in 1937.

Such a history does not sound propitious, and the

enormous success of the venture today is due partly to determination and largely to changing circumstances. It had an initial piece of good fortune, in that there were plans (which nearly reached fulfillment) for a long-distance footpath along the route of the track. This prevented it from being sold off piecemeal to the local farmers, and although the actual metal had been removed in the 1940s (as a war-effort gesture by the local authority), when the WHR company was finally formed in the 1960s, out of a splinter group from the Ffestiniog railway and other enthusiasts, at least the route, or most of it, was still available. The project started, however, with the core element of what is now the Welsh Highland Heritage Railway, now a separate company but formed of the then still-existing WHR Ltd., which now runs a museum and re-creation of the original Welsh Highland Railway over a one-mile track joined to the Porthmadog end of the WHR route.

The attitude of the Ffestiniog railway itself to the WHR enterprise was at first not as positive as it finally turned out to be. They bought it up from its residual owners, the receivers, with the intention of preventing the realisation of its plans. That was in the 1980s, but a change of policy in 1990 saw the Ffestiniog company committed to restoring the track, which they did in stages, starting in 1997. Now it runs the whole way from Caernarfon, further than the original, and with its spectacular journey through the Rhyd Ddu vallery, down to Beddgelert and through the lovely Aberglaslyn Pass, provides some of the best views possible of Welsh mountain scenery.

Completed in 2011, this is Porthmadog's newest asset, just as the pioneering Ffestiniog rail is its oldest. The town now has also turned back to its maritime roots, but in a lighter, recreational mood. You would not know that the background to the yacht harbour which now occupies some of the basin is something as momentous as the export of thousands of tons of slate. It is not now an essentially seaside town; the beach is at Morfa Bychan in the form of Black Rock Sands, but that is out of sight. Indeed there is even something of a clear division between the town and the harbour, an independence of the land and the sea.

Dolgellau

One of the defining qualities of Dolgellau is that it is a town associated with a mountain, like Chamonix, like Zermatt, like Grindelwald. In this case Cader Idris is not always visible from the town, but its presence is always felt, and much that is said about Dolgellau assumes that 'Cader' is one of the visitor's reasons for being there. Who was Idris, we may wonder, and why is this his seat?

The 'Triads of Britain' speak of 'Idris the Giant', and mention that he was a great astronomer; but this is considered unreliable testimony. The 'Annals of Wales' (by contrast) have him dying in 632, which does not sound like the same person. Neither version squares with the convention that he was a grandson of Cunedda, the northern chieftain who came to Wales in the late 5th century to help the native population rid themselves of the invading Irish. Cunedda is traditionally supposed to have come with eight sons, who gave their names to the regions of northern Wales. It must be said that it is probably the other way round: the names of the sons are a later invention to 'explain' the names of the regions.

Meirionydd is one such area, a *cantref* lying between the rivers Mawddach and Dyfi, absorbed into the county of Merionethshire under the Statute of Rhuddlan imposed by Edward I. Dolgellau was its county town, and was until the 1990s the administrative town of the district council (the district of Meirionydd being absorbed into Gwynedd after the Local Government Act of 1994). It was supposedly called after Meirion, son of Cunedda, and Idris was supposedly the son of Meirion.

*The bridge over the river Wnion forms both a historical
and a present feature of the town*

*Cymer Abbey, the beautiful ruins of which lie not far from Dolgellau
is one of the attractions recommended by travellers*

That it is not so simple need not too much concern us here. The fact is that the Latin document (a tenth century list of pedigrees) giving the information about Meirion is ambiguous, a basic confusion arising from the fact that two words for 'his' are used, both *eius* and *suus*, which might result in Meirion being Cunedda's grandson rather than his son. One would like to know, but the result does not materially affect the fact that both Meirion and Idris are connected with the colonisation by the northern tribe. This memory we have come across before, since the descent from Cunedda makes Idris a cousin of Maelgwn, the high king who ruled Gwynedd from Deganwy.

One other point about names arises, and that is the question of the name Dolgellau itself. It seems highly likely that it comes from the words *dol*, meadow, and *celli*, grove, so referring to the pleasantly varied pastoral and bosky nature of the setting; in which case the adoption of the present form (by the Rural District Council in 1958) is incorrect. The spelling of Welsh place-names has only recently become standardised, and throughout history has largely been a matter of personal choice – and 'Dolgellau' is no exception. In the 13th century it was spelt both Dolgelew and Dolgethley; Owain Glyndŵr himself spelt it Doguelli, Pennant Dolgelleu. The present form was adopted by the Church Registers in the 18th and 19th centuries and the District Council took it from there.

A point which arises incidentally from this is that there has been a village here for a remarkably long time. Such things are rare in northern Wales, where the nucleated settlement is something of an alien form, and the more usual pattern of place-identity is the 'township' of loosely associated farms which resulted from the breakup of the tribal holdings. Towns, even villages, are rarities in ancient Wales, but Dolgellau appears to have been a recognisable village since the 12th century. This would be more explicable if, like Caernarfon, it was based on a Roman foundation; but the Romans did not settle here, although they must have gone past this area on their way south from Tomen y Mur, the camp at Trawsfynydd, towards their next great nexus at Carmarthen. The exact route taken by Sarn Helen at this point is uncertain, but it may have looped round Cader Idris by veering east, a proposal supported by the existence of a minor Roman fort at Brithdir, not far from the modern road to Machynlleth and well to the east of Dolgellau.

Perhaps the strongest indication that Dolgellau was never a Roman settlement is its shape. The streets, wrote Pennant in the late 18th century, were *'disposed in a most irregular manner ...'* Bingley wrote, after his trip of 1798, that *'the streets are as irregular as it is possible to imagine them'*. Some attempt at pulling it together and joining up its little squares was made in the late 19th century, when it achieved some self-importance as a county town. But A.G Bradley wrote, in *Highways & Byways in North Wales* in 1909, *'nowadays it is a quaint and rambling collection of grey-walled slate-roofed houses ...'*

The travellers were generally grudging in their praise, directed at the setting rather than the town.

Pennant comments that it is small, *'but the situation is a beautiful vale, fertile, well wooded and embellished with numerous pretty seats ...'*, by which he perhaps meant the country houses round about, which Bradley also mentions: it is *'surrounded by leafy and attractive villas that the beauty of North Wales gathers round all such little towns'*. This situation is so appealing *'that it would be absurd to linger over its unpretentious architecture'*. That is the architecture noted by Bingley as in general *'low, and ill built'*.

All of them recognise that Dolgellau was essentially a gateway sort of place, the point of access to a much-favoured area. Bingley mentions *'interesting objects to the tourist as including (of course) Cader Idris, and three waterfalls, Rhiadr Du, The Fall of the Cain, and the Fall of the Mawddach'*. He recommends a visit to Cymer Abbey, still, as throughout Dolgellau's history, a major local feature. Bradley also considers that viewing other things is the main reason for being there: Cader Idris *'is generally the object of the traveller's attention'*. It is as well to note, in fairness, that a tourist base is far from being the only function which the town has had.

In fact Dolgellau has found itself several times at the focal point of international events.

Glyndŵr's war of independence, for instance, ebbed and flowed around it, largely because of the ambiguous position of the lords of Nannau nearby, and Henry Hotspur (as at the time Governor of North Wales) fought a battle outside the town on behalf of the king against Glyndŵr's supporters in 1401. It was not the unqualified success which he made out, and Hotspur soon afterwards changed sides. Perhaps this gave the Glyndŵr faction added confidence, and it is notable that by 1404 Dolgellau was a stronghold of the uprising.

Although Machynlleth is more famously associated with Glyndŵr's administration in his role as Prince of Wales, he did also hold a gathering of chiefs here, and from it issued an early call (in 1401) for support from the King of Scotland and the tribal chiefs of Ireland, both of which messages however failed to get delivered. The messengers were intercepted. More notable is the letter to Charles VI, king of France, on 10th May, 1404. This is often overshadowed by the more famous one written at the end of March 1406, that written from Pennal, a village beyond Cader Idris, which set out his ambitions for his nation. But the Dolgellau letter appears to have been seminal, in that it led directly to a treaty with France and the immediate dispatch of a fleet of sixty ships with seven hundred men to support Owain's cause. It was also in this letter from Dolgellau that he used his newly acknowledged title for the first time, '*Owynys dei gratia pinceps Wallie*'.

This means at least that something more than a village was here by the early 15th century, and indeed there is evidence for an identifiable place dating from Edward I's Survey of Meirionnydd, in 1253, when it was called Dolkelew. But it drops out of history for a bit after the involvement with Glyndŵr, and it only really appears on the world stage again in 1657, when it received a rather surprising but important visit.

Perhaps no more explanation for this is needed than that the town was on a route inevitably used by travellers passing between north and southern Wales. The bridge over the river Wnion was in place early, and essential to road traffic as not only did the river flood but the area around the town was marshy anyway. Pennant mentions the river, '*over which, on account of its floods, is a bridge of several arches*'. The bridge, Pont Fawr, still the only entry into the town from the north, was not new then, having been built in 1638. It is now part of an old road system which has been comprehensively by-passed, since at one time to go south from here you entered the town, dog-legged through its narrow streets, and emerged on a soaring country road up the flank of Cader Idris. Now traffic sweeps past it constrained in an almost underground system, the route of the defunct railway, before rising again, inevitably, around the mountain. The old bridge still reveals six arches, but is subdued at its northern end into the new road system, previously raised in order to pass over the railway, so now linking to the pass over the bypass; and to get into town at all by this route you have to do a curious, counter-intuitive, loop. You pass over the bridge unexpectedly now, without any of the old sensation of triumphantly entering Dolgellau.

Essentially Dolgellau is the focal point between this river crossing and the road which leads round Cader Idris and into mid Wales, on the one hand, the Roman road to Maridunum and now the A470 trunk route from north Wales to south; and on the other hand the focus also of the route which is the link to Welshpool and Shrewsbury and hence to England, the alternative London-to-Ireland route which was destined to be upstaged by that through Chester.

No wonder travellers found themselves stopping there. So it must have been by geographical chance that George Fox, with his colleague and travelling companion John-ap-John, coming from Tenby on his second journey into Wales, finding himself, via Pembroke and Haverfordwest, eventually in '*another county*', came to various places he can't remember by name, on his way to Beaumaris in Anglesey. '*A great market town*', and another '*great town*'. One of these was probably Machynlleth and the other Dolgellau. We certainly know, largely from the results, that he was there in 1657.

Fox had been brought up in the Puritan tradition, in Leicestershire, his father being a well-off weaver. He took it on himself at an early age to combat the established church, and ended by being something of a professional dissenter, preaching in popular places, such as town squares, to audiences which eventually could be counted in thousands. He must have been an impressive preacher, but at the time it was a dangerous thing to do, and Fox frequently found himself in jail. You could, at that time, be hauled before the magistrates for (for instance) wearing a hat in church, and Fox and his companion made a point of wearing their hats in church. This gesture was part of their message: ritual is of no importance. They were against hypocrisy in all its forms, and there was much of that about, from the corrupt misdirection of tithes to the exaggerated respect for education. They gained the nickname 'Quakers' through a remark made by a judge who mocked Fox's exhortation to tremble at the foot of the Lord.

He is thirty-three when we meet him, and has risen to be a power in the land. The year before, and earlier that year, 1657, he had had several long and probably influential meetings with Oliver Cromwell. The two got on evidently remarkably well – (though this did not eventually impede Fox's acceptance of the Restoration, which he took without opposition, in line with his radical pacificism). So when he came to Dolgellau, inevitably, on his way from southern Wales to Anglesey, his arrival would have been something of a major event, in this quiet but probably opinionated town.

That last assumption is derived by retrospection, since Dolgellau then showed itself, given its opportunity, to be remarkably strongminded. Judging again from subsequent evidence, Fox's principles of independence of mind, lack of pretention, lack of undue deference, found an echo in the social attitudes of Dolgellau. At any rate, though he was not there long, he made significant converts to Quakerism (the number is never exactly specified), and indeed so firmly rooted did it become, from that short encounter, that today there is a heritage centre dedicated to it, in the form of the upstairs of the Visitor Centre, at Tŷ Meirion, one end of Eldon Square, one of the town's old shops.

One of the converts made as a result of Fox's visit was a local farm-owner called Rowland Ellis, whose farm, called Bryn Mawr, can still be seen, up through the foothill country of primal moss-covered woodland above the town. It was one of the seemingly minor events which had repercussions larger than itself, but elsewhere. The Quakers of Dolgellau, like Quakers

The old farm of Bryn Mawr above Dolgellau gave its name to a district of Philadelphia and the famous girl's college.

The quaker George Fox

everywhere, were not left in peace to practise their new beliefs, but suffered systematic persecution.

The problem was that Quakers, basing their standpoint on a biblical prohibition of swearing oaths, refused to take the Oath of Allegiance, a matter of almost paranoid political importance after the Restoration. The Acts requiring this were initially intended to weed out Catholic 'recusants' from public office, but all who refused to take the oath became suspect of plotting against the crown, and the Quaker Act of 1662 was specifically aimed at ridding the country of organised dissenters. It made it explicitly illegal to refuse to take the Oath, which it was by implication anyway, and it added the burden that those who refused were not allowed to hold meetings, being now illegal persons. This Act was reinforced by the Conventicle Act of 1664, prohibiting secret meetings held by people not pledging allegiance to King and Country, which meetings now became criminal.

Quakers could now be found to be guilty of treason, and a court at Bala condemned some of them to be hanged, drawn and quartered, their women to be burnt, from which fate they were only rescued by intervention from a London lawyer, who arrived in time to show that this penalty was being prescribed by an out-of-date law. This poignant detail I owe to Marion Eames's invaluable notes, obtainable at the Dolgellau Visitor Centre.

One can see why, in the volatile circumstances, when much conspiracy was no doubt taking place, there was a fear of dissenting groups, opposed to the establishment in the form of the national church and the monarchy, who were prepared to place their religious beliefs ahead of their national allegiance: to the point when laws were made specifically to prohibit them – but it is much harder for us now, I think, to understand why this stalwart body of people held out in the face of almost certain imprisonment and the confiscation of goods, for what seems like a purely symbolic reason. Refusing to take the Oath of Allegiance is a way of conforming to ritual, we may feel, as much as would be the taking of the Oath.

Whatever the motives, the situation became so serious for these people in Dolgellau that they found it necessary to consider leaving. An opportunity happened to present itself at that time.

In March, 1681, Charles II gave a land charter of a large area of the New World to William Penn, in payment of a debt amounting to £16,000 which the king owed to Penn's father, an Admiral. It was the king who named it Pennsylvania, which Penn feared might be seen as his own self-aggrandisement; he insisted that the name should be seen as being in memory of his father. Penn, then aged thirty-seven, had converted to Quakerism in his twenties, and in fact went with George Fox, preaching their new faith, to Holland, in 1677. He instituted colonial government in his new territory, and one of the principles he imposed on it was freedom of religious belief. Quakers, persecuted as we have seen as illegal in Britain, were easily tempted to colonise this new, free, Quaker-friendly country. Rowland Ellis and his family were among them, and it is thus that a farm just outside Dolgellau gives its name to a town in Pennsylvania (now a suburb of Philadelphia) and a famous women's college, founded in 1885 and named after the town where it was set: Bryn Mawr. Originally a Quaker foundation, it had the distinction of being the first college to offer degrees to women, and remains much respected.

Confronted by events of such global importance the subsequent history of Dolgellau itself is likely to appear modest and parochial. Yet it always seems to have retained the knack of having repercussions in the greater world. The two periods of its separate success occurred about a hundred years apart but were otherwise quite unrelated to each other, both independent, both of limited period, and ultimately both curtailed by outside forces. Bingley reported, in the late 18th century, on the '*very considerable manufactories of flannel*' in the town, which he said '*from the number of hands necessarily employed*' had greatly increased the population compared to other Welsh towns. The main market, he said, was Shrewsbury, reminding us that what is different about Dolgellau, as a town on the edge of the Snowdonia National Park, is its focus on a different part of England.

The wool industry relied, in this case, on water power, and we are to see it as taking place not on the Wnion, Dolgellau's main river, but along the Aran, which still runs busily along the eastern side of the town, meeting the larger river in the area of green field upriver of the bridge. Here took place, in small but noisy mills, the activities to do with weaving, such as: fulling (compressing through beating, to close up the fibres of the cloth and make it compact); drying and bleaching; and earlier processes such as spinning and carding, which is a means of separating threads. All this reached a peak in about 1800.

Although the power came from water, the work was mainly done by hand, and Dolgellau's competitiveness in the market for woven wool was critically reduced by the rise of more fully mechanized woollen mills, with automated looms, during the early 19th century.

It was not long after the decline of the weaving industry that another, quite different, enterprise launched itself on Dolgellau. Rather surprisingly a belt of gold deposits runs in an arc of fifteen miles or so across the hills just north of Dogellau. There have been over time some sixty or so mines in this area, not many of them anything like successful. Gwynfynydd mine, Ganllwyd (now on the A470), was discovered in 1860 and active until 1998, producing more than 45,000 troy ounces of gold since 1884 – a troy ounce, called after Troyes in France, being a measure of precious metal equivalent to 1.09 ounces, or 31.1 grams. It was from here that the Queen was given an ingot on her sixtieth birthday, in April 1986, from which subsequent royal wedding rings have been made. More significantly for Dolgellau, Clogau mine near Bontddu, in the Barmouth direction, which had for a long time been producing lead and copper, moved into gold production in 1862 and started a gold rush, which actually was the second of three. The first Dolgellau gold rush, from 1854 to 5, had proved disappointing; the last, and best, was in 1887. This industry, supplied largely from Dolgellau, involved more than 500 miners at its peak around 1900. Clogau operated until 1911 and remained open to the public until 1998, producing 78,507 troy ounces from some 165,000 tons of gold.

It was the woollen trade, though, although historically limited, which had the most profound effect on the town, involving a lot of rebuilding and leading to its present appearance. The church, for instance, as it is at present, was an 18th century rebuilding, extended in 1864, of a 13th century original. Pennant mentions it as being the town's only remarkable building, containing (as it still does) the 14th century effigy of a member of the house of Nannau, Meurig Fychan, descendant of a prince and ancestor, as his name indicates, of the family of Vaughan. Dogellau was branching out commercially from its base in woven cloth. A printing press, for instance, was established there in 1798; and the presence of writers such as Bingley and Pennant is a symptom of something else which was going on, due to the establishment of the place as a posting point and a base for expeditions: the gradual transformation, during this period, of the 'picturesque travellers' (who came with pad and easel to try to record this scenery only recently recognised as Romantic), into what we would now recognise as tourists. The foundation of inns to serve them leaves another remnant of this period, though sadly the famous Golden Lion is at present (in 2011) closed. It was here that Bingley stayed, and in an early form of *TripAdvisor* he recorded his verdict:

> The best inn is the Golden Lion ... The provisions, except the wine, I found good; but the bed into which I was put was intolerable.

Eldon Square provides a rare area of focus in an otherwise largely unplanned town

Tŷ Siamas, a fine building in Eldon Square, has been through many public uses. Called after a local harpist, it now houses the Centre for Welsh Folk Music.

It is said that Wordsworth also stayed at the Golden Lion, and another comment on it in similar vein is (perhaps jokingly) attributed to him. Although this lacks verification, one somehow wishes the attribution to be true:

> If ever you go to Dolgelley
>   Don't stay at the Lion Hotel.
> You'll get nothing to put in your belly
>   And no-one will answer the bell.

Perhaps nothing better illustrates Dolgellau's self-confidence during the 19th century than the fine building on Eldon Square now known as Tŷ Siamas. It is the home now of the National Centre for Welsh Folk Music, a role which suits its history well, since it has been associated with local cultural activities almost since its construction, in the 1870s. As a Town Hall, assembly room, a market hall, a dance hall, it settled into use as a folk dancing centre, in the 1950s and 60s, and gradually fell into disuse, until it was refurbished and reopened in June 2007 in its current reincarnation as the National Centre for Welsh Folk Music, and entered a new period of both local and national importance, and with its present name of Tŷ Siamas – which respectfully commemorates an otherwise obscure local hero, Elis Sion Siamas, of nearby Llanfachraeth, who lived there in the late 17th and early 18th centuries: a harpist, said to have been one of the originators of the triple harp, and to have been the court harpist to Queen Anne. The triple harp, an instrument with three rows of strings, which came to be so strongly associated with Wales and

Welsh folk music that it is often referred to as the Welsh harp, was developed from the original instrument with a single row of strings, and had arrived in London from Italy during the early 17th century, coming to Wales from there via London-based Welsh harpists.

Somehow during this period of the town's flourishing, the 18th to 19th century, there came about a shift of perception by which what had been thought to be Dolgellau's defining flaw came to be seen as one of its main assets. It was not a planned town, not what the 18th and 19th centuries' preferences had come to view as the proper urban structure, a conformation to classical order; but rather an unfortunate collection of 'quaint and rambling' alleyways and irregular streets. We can now see (and during the 19th century people came to see this) that this form of cellular organic growth is a strength expressive of an integrated identity, here sturdily enforced by the consistent use of a local dolerite, originally rough and later dressed – a dark, coarse-grained, igneous rock.

Betws-y-coed

'Bed-hus'. Prayer house, in Old English. It is not uncommon among the names of Welsh villages, referring to an old religious site, perhaps originally the cell of the founding saint which in many cases became eventually the focal church of a village. One must assume that the name was given to the village by the invadcrs, and became in due course transliterated into Welsh. It is ironic that a Welsh place-name which now gives Anglo-phones something of a problem ('Betsi' is a frequent solution) turns out to be of Anglo-Saxon origin.

Betws-y-coed is cut off now from its ancient roots, being in its modern manifestation a trading complex along a through route, but it was originally the junction of several lines of infrastructure. It has, for instance, two rivers, going in different directions, though their joining point is not an evident feature of the town. The Conwy comes down its upper valley and into meadowland, surprisingly fat and amiable suddenly, after all its falls and cataracts. The Llugwy, more muscular, runs surging and gurgling under Pont y Pair. They join in the water-meadows down the valley a short distance north of Betws, and then, united as the Afon Conwy, proceed towards Llanrwst.

At Pont y Pair the old road along the east side of the valley joins the new road from Waterloo Bridge; but long before that the theme of roads and crossings had become established, when Sarn Helen, the Roman road from Canovium, crossed the Llugwy. It must be said that the exact route of Sarn Helen at this point is debated, and it

St Michael's, the 'prayer-house in the wood', which gives Betws-y-coed its name

The river Conwy flows peacefully alongside the town

may have varied during its period of use. The location of Caer Llugwy, a small Roman fort on the outskirts of Betws, indicates a more western route than the one traditionally supposed, which lies close to the Miners' Bridge, where workers from the settlement of Pentre Du, (the precursor of Betws-y-coed which still exists up the A5 where the road runs close to the river), crossed the Llugwy to go up to work (as people did until comparatively recently) in the lead mines in the hills above the northern side of the village.

John Cantrell and Arthur Rylance, in their book *Sarn Helen*, cite the Forestry Commision's publication about the Gwydir Forest as stating that the Roman road crossed the Llugwy fifty yards below the Miners' Bridge, and comment that it is more like one hundred yards, where '*the shallow crossing place can still be seen*'. The explanation for the rival crossing at Caer Llugwy, they point out, is that the fort here '*was occupied between 90 AD and 140 AD*' so that '*there were times when a march from Tomen y Mur to Caerhun would not involve a visit to Caer Llugwy*'.

It was the coming of the A5, of course, which changed the focus of Betws from these distant concerns. The coming of the railway had an even more radical, though less conspicuous effect: it cut the village off from its old church, the true, and eponymous, kernel of its one-time heart. Today there is a startling difference between the small bit of the town on the river Conwy side of the railway and the public confidence of the major resort the other side.

Old St Michael's sits squatly on a shelf over the river

The Roman road Sarn Helen crossed the Llugwy near the Miners' Bridge

The river Llugwy tumbles forcefully below Pont y Pair

bank, just above the suspension footbridge bridge which still connects the modern Betws with the eastern bank of the valley – the present structure built in 1930 to replace one washed away by a notable flood in 1928, itself built by soldiers during the Great War, the present one inheriting the local name of *Pont Soldiwrs*.

The old church is solidly established among its ancient tombs and monumental ewe trees, set back from the world in a micro-climate of vegetation, engulfed in the aromas of maturity, tree-guarded, as if to illustrate the second half of the town's name: the prayer-house in the wood. Indeed it seems from David Cox's famous painting of a funeral there, of 1848, that it has always been in a wood, not a village, connected to the world where people live by a long walled footpath.

Though the church is manifestly old, there are signs of an even older one. The font is considered to date from the 12th or early 13th century, and so was housed by a predecessor, since the oldest parts of the present building are 14th century. The Ancient Monuments Inventory indicates that the whole of the nave (which is undivided from the chancel) is of that century. The noble stone effigy of a knight which it houses, mentioned by Bingley who came in 1798, is in the late 14th century style, but although that might be contemporary with the church it has clearly been slightly trimmed to fit its present position. Part of its helmet has been cut. Bingley stopped here explicitly

to see an ancient monument in the church, in memory of Griffith, the son of David Goch, who was

Thomas Creswick's engraving of 1836 shows the village which the famous artists knew

a natural son of David , brother to Llewelyn, the last prince of Wales. He died in the fourteenth century, and is here represented by a large armed recumbent figure in a recess in the north wall.

Some of that is right. The effigy is that of Gruffudd son of Dafydd Goch, who died sometime between 1370 and 1380, who was a landowner in Penmachno and, through his wife, at Cwmllanerch, not far away from Betws in the Conwy valley. It is possible, as the guide book to the old church points out, that as a local landowner contemporary with the building of this church he was its patron, and hence came to end up in it in effigy. Records confirm that he fought at the battle of Poitiers under the Black Prince, in 1356, and some of the symbolism of the tomb suggests that he fell in battle – though it was probably not at that one, since he appears in another record locally in the 1350s. But it is not likely that he was a direct descendant of the last Prince. The line of Dafydd ap Gruffudd is generally thought to have died with him with his execution at Shrewsbury, and any descendant would have been prominent, and indeed a political threat, in the ensuing years.

St Michael's grew inadequate in the 19th century as the town expanded, and the congregation could not be contained in it. A north transept was added, in 1843, but this by itself could not deter the force of change. When the railway came, in the 1860s, the ancient footpath between the church and the village was effectively severed, and although a new Lychgate of this period seems to have been part of an initial attempt to reroute

David Cox's painting of a Welsh funeral shows the old church's woodland setting

The church contains a 12th or 13th century font

it, the forceful separation reinforced the feeling that Betws demanded, no doubt deserved, a prayerhouse more in keeping with the style of the times and the size of the town. In the course of this process St Michael's simply fell out of use, and was eventually declared redundant in 1996. It has not been deconsecrated, however, and services are still occasionally held there, though rarely. The care of the building is shared by the St Michael's Betws-y-coed Trust and the Friends of St Michael's.

There was evidently plenty of room, in 1873, to install the replacement church in some style. It lies in a comfortably open position, confident among huge cupressus, which are mature now in all their magnificence. We owe its fine quality, as we owe much else in Betws and the neighbourhood, to the ability and taste of a local, self-taught craftsman, Gethin Jones.

Gethin Jones was from Penmachno, born in 1816, his father being a stone mason; and indeed he was trained in that skill and only gradually worked his way up through the construction industry, to become a carpenter and then a builder, and finally a building contractor, in which role he influenced Betws and its area. He was, however, more than that, and as a poet and local historian survives in more than just stone buildings. He died in 1883 and his literary works were published the next year.

Gethin was much involved with the coming of the railway through Betws and on up the Lledr valley, building works for it as it progressed. The station at Llanrwst is one of his constructions, for instance, and in

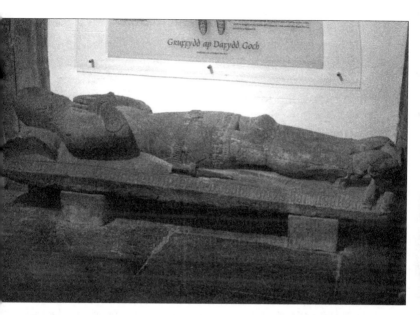

Griffydd ap Dafydd Goch

The old church contains the 14th century stone effigy of a local landowner – a descendant of the royal house of Gwynedd.

A lytch-gate appears to indicate a planned new route between the old church and the town

1868 he built Betws station itself, today something of a central feature in the visitors' experience. Most notably, when the track continued into the Lledr valley Jones undertook the long viaduct which carries it from one bank to the other of the Lledr, a magnificent mock-Gothic piece of stonework which still bears his name, Pont Gethin, Gethin's bridge.

Although it is Jones's expertise and craftsmanship which built the church, it was not in fact his design. A firm of architects was engaged, of Lancaster, and he, Gethin, made a loss on his contract.

By then, by 1873, the tiny village of Betws-y-coed had become fairly suddenly transformed. Its notable period, and to a large extent its claim to fame, lies in the immediately preceding years, from about 1840 to near the end of that century. Inevitably it is the name David Cox which remains central to this period, and the idea itself of the Betws-y-coed Artists Colony (the subject of an important book by the art historian Peter Lord) stems from him.

Cox was not a famous or particularly successful artist when he started painting Betws, although he exhibited at the Royal Academy from 1805, and his fame largely arose after his death. He was, for much of his career, a noted watercolourist, a member of what became the Water Colour Society since 1813. He supplemented his income from painting by teaching drawing. Only about 1840 did he change to oil painting, and exhibited in oil at the Royal Academy from 1844. He first came to Betws in 1805, and again the next year, and from 1844 until 1856 he spent every summer there.

The Royal Oak hotel was the base of the Betws-y-coed artists' colony in the 19th century

Cox was not of course the first person to paint this vividly romantic landscape. When Pennant came he brought with him Moses Griffiths, who provided the illustration for his 'Tours'. At the same time, the 1790s, Paul Sandby toured this area, and Turner himself came in 1798 and again in 1802. Thomas Roscoe produced a book of engravings of North Wales in 1836, to which Cox contributed, and set a definite trend by staying at the Royal Oak, which Cox subsequently made his base. As William Hall, a contemporary writer, describes it, it was a simpler building than in its later prime, '*a short, dark passage*' leading to '*the parlour, reserved for the company of "the higher order" ... Bacon and hams hung from the kitchen ceiling ...*' As Hall describes it the area was swamped with artists: their white tents and umbrellas '*to be seen in whichever direction the eye turned, suggested to the visitor the encampment of an invading army*'.

This indeed is the impression given too by Theodore Watts-Dunton in his romantic novel *Aylwin*:

On reaching Bettws y Coed I turned into the hotel there – 'The Royal Oak' ... I found the hotel full of English painters, whom the fine summer had attracted thither as usual ... Save myself, the guests were, I think, landscape painters to a man. They had been sketching in the neighbourhood. I thought I had never met so genial and good-natured a set of men ...

It is clear from the chronology that what had sparked this surge of attention, just as it has been the spring of

*The new church of 1873 was the work of
local contractor Gethin Jones*

*Gethin Jones was responsible for much construction near Betws during the railway age,
such as the viaduct over the Lledr called after him, Pont Gethin*

subsequent booms of different types, was the improvement of transport. Perhaps we can see the birth of it with the formation of the Capel Curig Turnpike Trust in 1802, which for the first time, by linking Lord Penrhyn's road from the coast near Bangor up to his quarries, now ran through to Capel Curig, providing a way into and through the mountains, where previously there had only been a perilous track. By 1808 (crucially for Betws-y-coed) the Shrewsbury to Holyhead mail-coach was using this, providing a route from London to Ireland which ran, for a long time, in competition with that through Chester. In 1811 Thomas Telford was commissioned to survey the road through northern Wales, and between 1815 and 1819 he undertook the improvement of the road which is now the A5. He included as a stretch of this the Capel Curig turnpike. In 1816 he built the Waterloo Bridge across the Conwy at Betws, and with that the town's destiny as a posting point on a through road was firmly set.

Before that Betws had been an unremarkable set of small buildings, a short stretch of cottages beautifully shown in Thomas Creswick's engraving of 1836, and indeed it remained so for some time. George Borrow, for instance, as comparatively late as the 1850s, went straight through it to the Swallow Falls without mentioning it at all, unless it is the '*neat dwellings for the accommodation of visitors*' which stand on the southern side of the pass into the hills. This is not much improvement on the place Bingley came past fifty years earlier, when he also went to the Swallow Falls, but also paused at Pont y Pair, '*not far from the village of Bettws*

The railway brought about a separation between the riverside setting of the old church and the expanding town

'Pont Soldiwrs' now is a 1930 replacement of a bridge across the Conwy from Betws built by servicemen during the Great War

y Coed'. As Bradley notes, and we have also mentioned, '*in Pennant's time there was practically nothing but the old church*'. But by the time he himself wrote, in the early years of the 20th century, that was a distant dream. '*Perhaps it was the passing stream of such travel that first opened out Bettws*' and by now, he said, it was '*not precisely the spot you would select in August for a quiet retreat*'.

One can feel taking place in the literature then the recognition of a transition which you get now with full force when you cross the railway, from the world of primal ecology and medieval certainty around the old prayerhouse, into the hubbub of coach party sociability which is a concomitant of the town's success the other side of the railway station.

*Telford's new through road for which the Waterloo Bridge
was built linked Betws with London*

The old stables of the Royal Oak Hotel – now a visitor's centre

Another view of the old parish church of St Michael's –
now in a quiet corner in the village of Betws-y-coed

Bibliography

Banholzer, K. F. *Old Carnarvon – Outside the Town Walls*, 2005.

Bingley, Rev. W., *North Wales*, Denbighshire County Council.

Borrow, George, *Wild Wales*, Oxford University Press, 1946.

Bradley, A. G., *Highways and Byways in North Wales*, Macmillan, 1909.

Cantrell, John and Rylance, Arthur, *Sarn Helen*, Cicerone, 1992.

Jenkins, J. Geraint, (trs. Martin Davies), *Welsh Ships and Sailing Men*, Gwasg Carreg Gwalch, 2006.

Lord, Peter, *The Betws-y-coed Artists' Colony*, National Library of Wales.

Pennant, Thomas, *Tours in Wales*, Caernarvon, 1883.

Watts-Dunton, T., *Aylwin*, Oxford University Press, 1921.

Further enjoyable reading on History and Heritage

Visit our website for further information:
www.carreg-gwalch.com

Orders can be placed on our
On-line Shop

Further enjoyable reading on Industrial Heritage

Visit our website for further information:
www.carreg-gwalch.com

Orders can be placed on our
On-line Shop

Further enjoyable reading on Snowdonia

Visit our website for further information:
www.carreg-gwalch.com

Orders can be placed on our
On-line Shop

Other books by the same author

Visit our website for further information:
www.carreg-gwalch.com

Orders can be placed on our
On-line Shop